Design   David West
                  Children's Book Design
Editor   Jen Green
Picture researcher   Cecilia Weston-Baker

The author, David Robins, is a research fellow at the center for Criminological Research, University of Oxford. He has written a number of studies of young offenders.

The consultant, Professor Jock Young, is principal lecturer in Criminology at Middlesex Polytechnic.

First published in
the United States in 1990 by
Gloucester Press
387 Park Avenue South
New York NY 10016

Printed in Belgium   All rights reserved

The publishers wish to acknowledge that the photographs reproduced in this book have been posed by models or obtained from photographic agencies.

Library of Congress Cataloging-in-Publication Data
Robins, David.
        Just Punishment / David Robins.
            p.   cm. -- (Understanding social issues)
        Summary: Surveys how justice is practiced in many different countries, and examines prison life and sentencing policies.
        ISBN 0-531-17252-X
        1. Corrections--Cross-cultural studies--Juvenile literature. [1. Corrections. 2. Punishment. 3. Prisons.]
        I. Title. II. Series.
        HV9443.R63   1990
        364.6--dc20   90-3220   CIP   AC

CONTENTS

UNDERSTANDING SOCIAL ISSUES

JUST PUNISHMENT

David Robins

GLOUCESTER PRESS
London : New York : Toronto : Sydney

The way society punishes people reflects our own values and attitudes. The riot at Strangeways prison in Manchester, England, in April 1990 exposed the horrors of the prison system. Normally this is something most of us would prefer not to think about too deeply.

The reasons why people commit crimes are complicated. Some commit crimes because they are unemployed and penniless. Others turn to crime while at work – the cashier who pilfers from the till, the business fraudster.

There is no single explanation for what causes crime. There is also no single solution. Some believe that the punishment should fit the crime. But the reality is rarely so straightforward. As well as looking at ways of making people pay for their crime we should also be looking at practical ways of helping people who do get into trouble. What can be done with a teenager who is constantly involved in petty crime? How can he or she be got out of an increasingly nasty cycle of crime and personal unhappiness? Punishment is not simple. It is often a dangerous idea. We should remember that in many countries legal punishments are used to crush opposition to unpopular governments.

This book draws on examples of punishment from around the world. It looks at how we decide on punishment, the reasons why we choose to punish people, who gets punished, and the methods of punishment employed in different societies. This book questions whether punishment is always the best way to deal with law-breakers. It may help you decide what is "just" punishment. There are no easy answers.

The riots at Strangeways and other British prisons in 1990 were the latest in a series of violent incidents in British jails. Overcrowding was blamed as the main factor leading to the crisis. Britain has a higher percentage of its population in prison than any other European country.

CHAPTER 1

CRIME AND PUNISHMENT

The old village
lockup in
Litlington,
Cambridgeshire,
England. The
imprisonment of
offenders to
punish them and
protect society
has been
practiced for
hundreds of
years.

Everyone knows what a "crime" is: according to the Oxford English Dictionary, it is an "act punishable by law." But people usually associate the word "crime" with the more sensational and serious offenses – the ones that hit the headlines, such as murder, manslaughter, and armed robbery. We often forget that such petty offenses as careless driving, parking violations, and dropping litter on the street are also crimes. The only real difference is in the severity of punishment for different offenses.

The same principles apply to mass murderers as to shoplifters and fare dodgers. In the eyes of the law a crime is a crime – however serious or trivial the offense may be. But the murderer is likely to be treated far more harshly than the shoplifter because his action is more harmful to society.

We are all potential offenders. Criminal behavior is not some evil alien force. It may arise out of our ordinary daily affairs. The routine methods of running a business may contain their share of "illegal" activities. For some people, making a living or practicing a trade means cutting legal corners if they are to survive. Many of the things we take for granted in our daily personal lives are, strictly speaking, illegal.

Until very recently, however, it was generally accepted that criminals were completely depraved people and that their illegal behavior was immoral. The obvious reaction of society, therefore, was to punish them. If they are punished severely enough, so the old argument runs, wicked people mend their ways and conform to ordinary decent standards of behavior. This simple belief about the nature of crime and punishment has survived for thousands of years and is still far from dead. But punishment is extremely limited. It is true that the majority of generally law-abiding citizens can be restrained from committing minor offenses by fear of the consequences. But more serious offenders will not "learn" by being disciplined in this simple, schoolboy way.

Many offenders see the results of punishment as less serious than the potential rewards of law-breaking. Some offenders have little to lose by going on trial and being convicted. Attempts by society to punish other offenders may simply satisfy their belief that society is against them.

People's reactions to punishment, then, vary greatly. Consider two types of driving offenders. Both love driving at high speeds. Driver A is stopped by the police and fined $160. The result is that the next time his foot presses down too far on the accelerator he remembers how much it cost him last time, and resists the temptation.

Driver B, on the other hand, is completely addicted to speed. No amount of fines and police warnings can kill her addiction. She may end up either killing herself, or, as many do, killing someone else. This example shows that the effectiveness of punishment is not always so simple.

"Longer sentences don't serve as deterrents. These guys are in here because they didn't think they'd get caught." Prison Superintendent Paul Delo of Potosi Missouri Correctional Center.

CHAPTER 2

WHO DECIDES?

A British high
court judge. In
many countries
including Britain
and the United
States, the
verdict of the trial
is determined by
the jury, after
which the judge
pronounces
sentence on
offenders.

Trial by jury

Many countries have different ways of deciding who has broken the law and how they should be punished. For minor offenses most societies have a system of small local courts operated by magistrates, whose job is to decide whether the defendant is guilty and, if so, to determine his or her punishment. For more serious cases, many countries, including the United States and Britain, operate the jury system. The idea of the jury system is quite simple. The outcome of the trial is determined by citizens, not by governments, judges or other powerful interests who may have their own axe to grind.

> **"The object of any tyrant would be to overthrow trial by jury. Trial by jury is the lamp that shows that freedom lives."** Lord Devlin, House of Lords judge.

A typical jury consists of 12 ordinary citizens who can be relied upon to hear a case in a fair and unbiased way. Anyone between the ages of 18 and 65 can be called to jury service. Some people are excused jury service because of personal difficulties or because they may be biased. Police, prison officers, lawyers, and those who work in the legal system, for example, are not allowed to serve on a jury.

The job of a jury is to decide if a defendant is innocent or guilty. If a person is acquitted (found not guilty) by a jury, he or she is released and that is the end of the case. But if a person is found guilty, the jury does not usually decide the punishment. In the United States six states allow the jury to sentence a convicted felon. Elsewhere decisions about punishment are left to the judge, although juries may make their views known. First the judge will ask the police what is known about the prisoner. He may ask for details of the prisoner's criminal record. Or he may hear speeches on the prisoner's behalf from his or her lawyers. They would normally be asking for a light sentence. If he cannot immediately make up his mind, the judge may well adjourn or delay the case, so that further reports can be prepared on the prisoner's background.

The jury system is not perfect. In complicated fraud cases, for example, or cases in which there is

The violent attack by Liverpool fans on Juventus fans at the Heysel stadium in Brussels in 1985 was the most serious instance of soccer hooliganism in recent years. The just punishment of those responsible became a matter of international concern.

a lot of scientific and technical evidence, a committee of specially qualified experts might be better suited to come to a verdict or judgment. Juries can also be tampered with occasionally. Bribes may be offered to jury members by friends of the defendant to "persuade" them to press for a verdict of not guilty. Jury members may be threatened with violence. This has happened during trials of members of the Mafia, the powerful criminal organization that flourishes in the United States and Italy. In Mafia cases it is often hard to pick a jury which is not frightened.

But for all its faults, the jury system is an *independent* way of making judgments. The evidence of judicial systems around the world is that justice suffers when the jury system is suspended or abolished and governments and other powerful interests take over the functions of the law.

Offenders are not always treated alike in the courts. Sentences can vary greatly from court to court – and from judge to judge. Research shows that in general sentences are likely to be harsher when set by a jury than when decided by a judge. By pleading guilty, offenders are likely to get their sentences halved. Pleading guilty to a felony (crime) boosts the odds of staying out of prison. A U.S. Justice Department study reports that of those defendants who plead guilty, often as the result of a plea bargain, only 65 percent go to prison. The other 35 percent are usually put on probation.

Internment
During the early seventies, the British government became increasingly worried about the growth of

the Irish Republican Army (IRA) and other terrorist organizations in Northern Ireland. In August 1971, "internment" was introduced in Northern Ireland. Internment meant that people who the authorities felt were "a serious threat to public order" could be picked up by the police and the army and held without trial. Internment was a very serious step. It meant that people's normal legal rights, the right to trial by jury, for example, had been abolished. When the first 300 people were detained in the Maze Prison in Belfast, riots broke out in many cities in Northern Ireland.

State of emergency
When governments feel threatened by growing unrest they often take emergency powers. In 1985 a state of emergency was declared by the government of South Africa after riots engulfed black townships throughout the country. In 1989 martial law was declared in China, after a series of peaceful demonstrations by students opposed to the government were crushed by army tanks in Tiananmen Square in Beijing, the Chinese capital.

Military courts, and other courts with "special powers," exist in many other countries, including Iraq, Israel, Ethiopia, and the Sudan. Often people are severely punished simply because they are opposed to the government. They are not allowed a fair trial. Amnesty International is a worldwide organization that campaigns on behalf of the thousands of "prisoners of conscience" from many countries whose only "crime" is that their views differ from those of the government.

CHAPTER 3

WHY PUNISH?

A prisoner in an isolation cell in Boniato prison, Cuba, considers his next chess move. Solitary confinement is practiced in prisons throughout the world to punish offenders for infringement of prison rules.

The idea that would-be lawbreakers will think twice if you make an example of one of them is one of the oldest and most common reasons for especially severe treatment of offenders. But does harsh punishment really deter?

Paul Storey and the Handsworth mugging

In November 1972, James Keenan was walking home in the Handsworth area of Birmingham, England. Three boys appeared out of the shadows, knocked him to the ground and dragged him half conscious to a nearby uninhabited area where they robbed him of a small amount of money. A couple of hours later they returned to the same spot, and, finding their victim still lying on the ground, they

Inmates of a Young Offender Institution in Britain. Are such establishments effective in rehabilitating juvenile lawbreakers, or do they serve as "universities of crime?"

attacked him again. Two of the boys kicked him, while one, Paul Storey, hit him with a brick. Keenan's injuries were extremely serious. Some months later the case came to court, and its outcome shocked everyone. The judge told Paul Storey, "You are nothing more or less than a wild animal." Paul Storey was sentenced to 20 years' imprisonment. He was 16 at the time of the offense.

Many people supported the judge's action. To them the sentence on Paul Storey was a sign that society had "had enough" of youthful lawlessness, and was prepared to "get tough" and "stand firm."

The case took place at a time of increasing public concern in Britain about the growing number of street robberies and muggings. But many other people were deeply opposed to the sentence. They argued that to lock a 16-year-old boy away for so long was inhuman. They accused the judge of playing up to public fears. The Paul Storey case shows how public opinion plays an important part in society's treatment of offenders. But did the severe sentence passed on Paul Storey deter potential young muggers? There is no evidence that the treatment of Paul Storey had any effect on the levels of street robberies in Britain.

Does punishment deter?

There is little evidence that harsh punishment deters criminals. To combat a growing drug menace, for example, China, Malaysia, Iran, and several other countries have executed thousands of people involved in the drug trade. But even these harsh measures have had only a limited effect. The financial rewards are so great that drug dealers may even see the threat of being hanged as a risk which is worth taking.

When life means life

In 1979 the state of Missouri brought back the death penalty and other harsh sentences for first degree murder. This included life terms without parole – in other words, the sentencing of convicted murderers to jail with no prospect of a reduced sentence for good behavior.

This "lock 'em up and throw away the key" approach proved popular with the public. Many argued that depriving dangerous people of even the hope of release is the best way to provide effective protection for society. But the problem is, what to do with a growing number of men whose only hope of leaving prison is in a coffin?

Potosi Missouri Correctional Center houses 461 inmates, two-thirds of whom are in for life without parole. Prison staff try to keep them involved in programs of work, athletics, and education. Meanwhile, the inmates grow older. The over-45s are the fastest-growing segment of Potosi's population. In Potosi the cost of maintaining these "senior citizens" in prison is enormous: $35 per person per day. Maximum security prisons are also expensive to build – Potosi cost $55 million, and taxpayers in Missouri are reluctant to pick up the bill. This leaves the prospect of dangerously overcrowded prisons, filled with hardened lifers with nothing left to lose – a situation that many feel is a recipe for violence. Officials in Missouri and around the country are beginning to wonder if "show no mercy" sentencing is such a great idea.

Martyr to freedom

In some countries opponents of the dominant regime are given heavy sentences to deter others. But sometimes this can have quite the opposite effect. Perhaps the most famous example of this is the imprisonment of Nelson Mandela. In June 1964, Mandela, a black South African lawyer, was sentenced to life imprisonment by a South African Court. He had been found guilty of attempting the violent overthrow of the white supremacist government. Mandela was to spend the next 26 years in prison. During this time he became a symbol of black South Africans' struggle for freedom from the injustice of apartheid.

When Mandela first entered prison, few people

By the time of his release from custody in South Africa in 1990, the case of ANC activist Nelson Mandela had been taken up by pressure groups all around the world, and his name had become synonymous with the struggle against apartheid.

outside South Africa had heard of him. Yet when he was finally released in February 1990, following enormous pressure from the world community, he was immediately recognized internationally as the leader of black South Africa.

Vigilante law

Vigilantes is the name given in the United States to self-appointed groups of people who take it upon themselves to mete out justice. In the history of the Wild West, vigilante committees were common in communities where the laws that governed the rest of the United States were yet to be established. In place of a process of arrest, trial and sentence by a properly convened court of law, vigilantes substituted their own "kangaroo courts." In their haste to "string 'em up and be damned of the consequences," the activities of vigilante groups were often themselves serious criminal acts.

Perhaps the most notorious of vigilante groups was the Ku Klux Klan, who sprang up in the southern states of America after their defeat in the Civil War. Their attempt to preserve white supremacy resulted in thousands of black people being lynched and burned. As the activities of the Klan subsided, racial prejudice remained. Research has suggested that up until quite recently some of the death sentences passed on blacks in southern courts were little more than legal lynchings.

Make my day!

In the 1960s, as courts throughout the United States attempted to become more humane in their methods, frustration grew among the general public. Revenge movies with vigilante heroes became enormously popular. In the film *Death Wish* Charles Bronson plays an ordinary guy whose family falls prey to vicious muggers, and who decides to take the law into his own hands. In *Dirty Harry* Clint Eastwood plays a tough cop whose partner is killed by a hit-and-run driver. He is determined to show no mercy to evil-doers, who are constantly being put back on the streets by "soft" judges. Dirty Harry's approach is more basic and brutal. "Come on punk, make my day!"

The subway vigilante
Films like *Dirty Harry* and *Death Wish* are entertaining fantasies. They have little to do with the reality of life in a complex society with a high crime rate like the United States. But in December 1984, the fantasy threatened to become a reality. Bernhard Goetz, a young white electrician, was riding a New York subway train when he was approached by four black teenagers. They asked him for five dollars. With the words, "Here's five dollars for each of you," Goetz calmly took out a pistol and shot all four. Goetz was later arrested and charged with attempted murder. But to thousands of frustrated New Yorkers Goetz had become an overnight hero, a real life Charles Bronson. Goetz was dubbed "The Subway Vigilante."

Goetz's defenders insisted that his action was justifiable. He had used a weapon to protect himself from a threat to his life, they argued, and therefore should not have been charged with any crime.

But others were less sure. They pointed out that the case was far more complex than it appeared. At no time was Goetz threatened with a weapon. Did the teenagers intend to rob Goetz or were they simply begging for money? There was also the suggestion that much of the support for Goetz was white racism in disguise.

In June 1987, Bernhard Goetz was finally cleared of attempted murder by a New York court, but served six months in jail for carrying a gun without a license. A quiet, unassuming character, Goetz himself was no Charles Bronson.

But the Subway Vigilante had made his mark. In New York a self-appointed group of crime fighters, the Guardian Angels, ride the subways. The Angels are opposed to instant justice. Would-be muggers and others are handed over to the police. But the widespread support for the Guardian Angels reflects the frustration many feel about the authorities' apparent inability to halt the rising tide of crime.

An eye for an eye

There are those who support harsh punishment for offenders because they believe in retribution. Retribution means that those who take human life must expect to pay with their own.

The idea of retributive justice is as old as the Bible, and is still powerful. Retributionists have helped the return of the death penalty in many parts of the United States, despite the strong evidence that even when the death penalty is in force, the number of murders still continues to increase.

Divine justice? The Rushdie affair

Sometimes punishment based on religious law conflicts with laws made by society.

In February 1989, Ayatollah Khomeini, the Iranian leader, ordered the execution of Salman Rushdie, the British-based author. Rushdie had been accused of blaspheming the Islamic religion by insulting the prophet Mohammed in his novel *The Satanic Verses*. In a "fatwa," or decree, broadcast on Teheran radio, the Ayatollah informed the Moslem people of the world that the author, together with those involved in the publication of his book who were aware of its content, were all sentenced to death. After Khomeini's fatwa, there were anti-Rushdie riots, and copies of the book were publicly burned along with effigies of its author. Salman Rushdie has since been forced to live in hiding with a strong police guard, and may need protection for the rest of his life.

Many Moslems deplore Khomeini's fatwa. They point to the need for compassion and mercy toward wrongdoers. Others argue that although "death is the just punishment for the blasphemer," Moslems must respect the laws of non-Moslemic societies. But many others support Khomeini's sentence, claiming his fatwa is the true voice of Islamic justice.

The Rushdie case shows how for many people throughout the world the laws of God are more important than the laws of people. To them, divine retribution is the justice which society should demand.

CHAPTER 4

WHO GETS PUNISHED?

Convicted young offenders in an Institution yard. In Britain the peak age for offending is 15, and one quarter of all crime is committed by juveniles – people under the age of 18.

In theory a criminal justice system should not be concerned with whether you are a man or a woman, black or white, young or old, rich or poor. Indeed the idea that all of us are equal in the eyes of the law is often held up as one of the most important principles of a civilized society. But are we really all equal before the law? Close inspection reveals that this idea is something of a myth. In reality the law treats different categories of people in very different ways.

Women in prison – a fair deal?

Women have special problems in the criminal justice system. There are far fewer women in prison than men. But this does not mean that they are dealt with more fairly. Women who get sent to prison often face extra hardships just because they are women.

The values and attitudes which motivate most prison systems are very largely male ones. According to one writer, Shirley Cooklin, the male emphasis on discipline and conformity in prisons is alien to most women, who find it harder to cope, possibly without even knowing why. Indeed this is now officially recognized in that women no longer have to wear uniforms in British prisons.

The effect of going to prison may also be greater on women than men. Men who have "done time" often acquire a macho image. The vast majority of women who go to prison, like the majority of men, come from the poorest sections of society. Most women who receive a "custodial sentence" are convicted of minor, nonviolent first offenses. A large number of women prisoners are there

Mothers serving time at Askham Grange women's prison in Britain are trained in childcare. The number of women in prison in the United States has doubled in five years to 40,000. Three-quarters of the women are mothers.

because they have been given a fine that they cannot afford to pay.

Alternatives to a prison sentence – community service for example – are less likely to be offered to women first offenders than to men. Women's prisons are often harsh and rigid places. Research has shown that women prisoners are more than twice as likely to be disciplined while in prison than men are.

Tranquilizing drugs and other powerful sedatives are used more widely on women prisoners than on men. Women inmates include some who are mentally disturbed. The extra stress placed on women by prison can cause women "to suffer more than men from the emotional strain of imprisonment and separation from their families."

The location of women's prisons also causes problems. Because there are fewer women prisoners than men, there are fewer women's prisons. This means that women are more likely than men to be sent to an establishment a long way from home. This can result in fewer visits from family and friends, and a greater feeling of isolation and hopelessness.

Locking up babies
Punishing women by sending them to prison often means that young children are punished too. Women are still mainly responsible for child care. When a prisoner is a mother, the problem is very real, especially if she is a single parent. Many people believe that to lock up a pregnant women is barbaric. But there have been several cases of this. In one case the judge sent a young mother to

prison with her newborn baby. (They were eventually released following a public outcry). In this way children can become innocent victims of society's desire to punish wrongdoers by sending them to prison.

Black people

The evidence is that black people are treated differently in the criminal justice system. Research has shown that they are more likely to be stopped and searched on the streets, more likely to be arrested and charged if they are first offenders, rather than cautioned, and more likely to be imprisoned. Black people are also more likely to be the victims of crime.

Members of the Jamaican-based criminal network the Yardies. In Britain the record of the treatment of black people is poor, and the number of black police and prison officers is tiny.

Ghetto justice

In the United States you are most likely to be at the receiving end of the justice system if you are young, black and poor. But what is less often remembered is that this group is also most likely to be the victims of crime.

> **"In the ghetto I see a new generation of cocaine kids in faded jeans and unlaced sneakers, draped with gold chains, their arrow-pointed haircuts topping fresh faces and hard-edged frowns. These kids are grown before their time, wise before they leave home, smart before they go to school, rule-breakers before they know the rules, and lawbreakers after they know the law.**
>
> **"The innocence of the young is lost in Washington Heights [in New York City] as a new generation of street corner boys and girls enter the shadowy world of dealing and prostitution."** Terry Williams, *The Cocaine Kids* (Addison-Wesley, 1989).

It is estimated that the United States has 5.3 million poor, inner city children. "These children are surrounded by a very real and immediate world of violence, of gunfire, of death," says Theadore Cron, special assistant to the U.S. Surgeon General. "It's every day. We simply didn't have that before."

CASE STUDY

Lafayette Walton is twelve years old. He lives in a public housing project in Chicago, a seven-block stretch of red-brick apartment buildings on the city's West Side.

Lafayette lives in a neighborhood where gunshots are as common as the playful laughter of young children. He has watched men being beaten, and has seen family friends shot. Two bullet holes in the curtains of his family's apartment are reminders of a gang shoot out. When he was ten, Lafayette stood over a dying teenager who had been gunned down by a rival. Not long before Lafayette's twelfth birthday, his mother permanently lost the use of two fingers when she was attacked by knife-wielding muggers.

During the summer in Lafayette's neighborhood, an average of one person every three days is beaten, shot at or stabbed. Gang warfare is often over control of the illegal drug trade. When the sound of gunfire fills the air, Lafayette's mother hurriedly herds the younger children onto the floor of their apartment. Through the window they catch glimpses of young gunmen, waving their pistols about. One youth totes a submachine gun. In an apartment upstairs, other gang members blast away at rivals in a building across the street. Some of these "soldiers" are as young as 13.

Lafayette has been caught up in gang wars since he was a small child. It is possible that he himself will become a "hardened offender." Some argue that the fault lies in the juvenile justice system, which, it is sometimes claimed, is too lenient with young criminals. Others point to the unemployment, poor housing and education, and broken families that typify Lafayette's neighborhood. If Lafayette wants to "go straight" he will have to overcome these disadvantages. In the poor neighborhoods of Chicago, nearly 300 children are shot every year. Lafayette is a victim of the kind of social conditions that breed these crimes. Punishment on its own cannot be the solution.

CHAPTER 5

METHODS OF PUNISHMENT

Every country in the world has prisons, and they may be a necessary evil, although there are movements lobbying to abolish them entirely in Germany and Scandinavia. It is debatable whether the effect of prison on offenders is in the long-term interests of society.

Fine

The fine is by far the most common method of punishing people who commit minor crimes. In the United States and Britain over 80 percent of sentences carried out in the lower courts are fines. If an offender is wealthy this can affect the amount of a fine he or she would have to pay. But whether the offender is rich or poor is not meant to influence the judge's basic decision of whether or not to fine him or her.

> **"The way you end business fraud, embezzlement and corruption is to scare the daylights out of the criminals who wear suits and ties, by putting 'em in the slammer with the bank robbers!"** United States district attorney, remarking on a fraud case he helped bring to court.

For a long time fines were felt to be the proper way to deal with white-collar crimes – criminal acts related to an offender's job or profession. But the cost of fraud has grown in recent years. Sometimes the amounts of money gained from a business fraud can make the proceeds of the average bank robbery seem small by comparison. Yet the bank robber's crime is more public; he is more likely to make the news, and if caught, to go to prison.

Times are changing. Recently a bank official who made off with $30 million was sentenced to two concurrent (to be served one after the other) 20-year jail terms. Americans suffer losses of more than $40 billion a year from this kind of crime: far, far more than from violent bank robberies.

> "How can the law be fair? How do you fine a person enough who can earn more in a week than the average guy earns in a whole year?" Police Officer.

Can't pay, won't pay

There are limits to the amounts judges can impose as fines. The court can also allow fines to be paid off by weekly installments. An offender who wants "time to pay" has to show evidence of how much he or she earns or receives in welfare benefits, and how much family commitments or basic living expenses amount to.

The majority of people who appear before the courts are poor and often unemployed. Far from deterring them from crime, the pressure to pay up "otherwise you go to prison" can force them into more crime. Fines imposed on so-called white collar criminals, on the other hand, are often negligible considering their personal wealth. For example, a fine of $1,700 with costs for dangerous driving recently passed on a millionaire was condemned by many as "peanuts." Of course, if he had been an unemployed teenager the fine would have been attacked as too severe.

> "It's the rich what gets the pleasure
> It's the poor what gets the blame." Old Cockney music hall song.

To get around the problems of fining the poor, courts can sometimes make fine supervision orders, which require the offender to be placed under the care of a probation officer who can

White-collar criminals are usually punished by the imposition of fines. But some US public officials feel that prison sentences should be imposed on business fraudsters, and this is proving a popular vote-winner.

encourage the offender to sort out his or her financial affairs. He or she can then pay off the fine in a series of installments.

> "In poor neighborhoods the police protect the people from the thieves. In rich neighborhoods the police protect the thieves from the people." Old saying.

If all else fails, whether rich or poor, the offender who does not pay the fine can be sent to prison. In general, the more the offender owes the court, the longer the term of imprisonment is likely to be. In Britain during 1988 nearly one quarter of all those sentenced to prison were fine defaulters.

Absolute discharge

Sometimes a court may feel that it would be wrong to punish a convicted person. If so the person may receive an absolute discharge or release. For example, the driver of a fire engine hurrying to an emergency might pass through a traffic stop sign. Technically he is guilty, but the court may feel that it would be unfair to punish him.

Another recent example of an absolute discharge is less clear-cut. An elderly man administers a lethal poison to his aged wife at her request. The court hears that she was terminally ill and in dreadful pain. Although they are technically guilty of murder, many courts are reluctant to punish people involved in such tragic cases. Often an absolute discharge is the verdict. But such cases do raise the important issue of whether or not it can *ever* be right for one person to deliberately take the life of another.

Prison

All prisons are intended to deprive people of their freedom, although the way this is done may vary from country to country.

There are usually strict rules which govern the sending of people to prison. Most offenses have a fixed maximum prison sentence attached to them. But often offenders will receive less than the maximum. There is also the possibility of one-third off their sentence for good behavior.

Prisons are supposed to be "the last resort." There are also many other variations of sentence which a judge can impose which do not involve an immediate prison sentence. These include a suspended sentence, whereby a person is sentenced to prison, but the sentence will not come into effect if the offender behaves him- or herself for a fixed period. There is also the conditional discharge, whereby a conviction will stand, but the offender will be released without punishment. If any other offense is committed then he or she may be brought back to court and given a sentence which may include prison.

Improving prisons
Many prisons are staffed by forward-looking people, who encourage extensive education and training programs for prisoners, especially young offenders. In young-offender institutions in Britain, the emphasis is on a mixed program of work, study, sports, and physical education. Prisons such as Grendon near Birmingham provide special psychiatric help for prisoners convicted of serious or violent crimes. The Special Unit at Barlinnie in Scotland has been successful in helping to reform inmates who were once considered "hopeless lifers."

Many prisons have a relaxed and open approach. In Holland, inmates have their own rooms, wear their own clothes and can hire televisions or even CD players. In Sweden and Denmark prisoners are allowed private visits from their wives. Conjugal visits are also allowed in one Corsican prison.

Prisons can be improved and made more humane and efficient. But the overwhelming evidence is that in general, prisons fail to rehabilitate or reform people, nor do they deter them from crime.

Prison punishment

There are prisons within prisons. Sex offenders and other unpopular categories of offenders are often kept segregated from other inmates for their own safety. There are also maximum-security blocks that house prisoners considered especially dangerous and high-risk, who are separated from the rest of the prison population. In the United States, electronic surveillance keeps maximum-security inmates under constant watch.

If a prisoner infringes prison rules he or she can be sent to solitary confinement for long periods of time. In West Germany, a "silent wing" was set up to punish rebellious prisoners by depriving them of all sound.

Many prisoners complain of the overcrowding, boredom and pointlessness of life "inside."

"You are sent to prison as a punishment, not to be punished. Unfortunately, that is what happens most of the time." Ex-prisoner.

Prisons in crisis

The horrors of the riots at Strangeways and other British prisons during the spring of 1990 are part of a long and violent history of prison revolt. In the United States during the 1960s and 1970s, violent uprisings in prisons in New Mexico, California and New York State cost hundreds of lives.

There have been serious disturbances in British prisons throughout the 1980s. Violent outbreaks have also occurred in prisons in France, Italy, and

Yugoslavia. In 1974 in France prisoners in 77 establishments went on the rampage, leaving nine inmates dead.

What now for prisons?

On death row in San Quentin jail, California. Does the state have the right to take human life? The rights group Amnesty International has expressed growing concern about the use of capital punishment throughout the world.

These disturbances have increased the public's disillusionment over the amount of money spent locking up more and more people and the evidence of how little it achieves. Meanwhile, the number of prisoners throughout the world continues to grow, and many prisons are hopelessly overcrowded.

Combatting the prison culture

The urgent need, according to Vivien Stern of the British National Association for the Care and

Resettlement of Offenders (NACRO), is to tackle the culture of violence that has grown up within the prison system.

"The notion of violence is deeply embedded," she says. "It is accepted that prisoners will exert violence on each other and – whether they really are or not – that they will be treated violently by the staff. The staff expect violence from the inmates. You have got to change that basic premise, and the way to do it is to introduce smaller living areas with purposeful activities. The inmates will have everything to lose by smashing the place up. It makes obvious common sense, but it has hardly begun to happen."

The death penalty debate
The death penalty, or capital punishment, is the most controversial of all legal punishments. In the United States 36 states permit the death penalty. By May 1990 the number of prisoners under sentence of death had risen to 2,326. Some 922 (42.6 percent) were black, 1,174 (50.5 percent) white, and the remaining 6.9 percent were from other ethnic minority groups.

Between January and August 1989, 13 prisoners were executed in eight states: three in Alabama, two in Florida, Nevada, and Texas, and one each in Georgia, Mississippi, Missouri, and Virginia. They included one Vietnam veteran who was believed to have been emotionally disturbed following his experiences in the war. Two black prisoners executed had been convicted and sentenced to death by all-white juries in districts with a large black population.

Polls show that the death sentence is popular with the public. One does not have to look very far for one of the reasons. During 1988, 20,675 homicides were reported in the United States.

The case of Horace Dunkins

In June 1989, the United States Supreme Court ruled by five votes to four that the execution of mentally retarded defendants was permissable under the Constitution. Following this decision, in July 1989, Horace Dunkins was executed in Alabama despite evidence suggesting that his IQ was about 65 and his reasoning ability that of a young child. At least seven other prisoners executed in recent years are believed to have been mentally retarded.

"There are laws to punish us. But where are the laws to protect us?" Political prisoner.

Executing juveniles

The U.S. Supreme Court has also ruled that juveniles may be executed. The youngest offender to be sentenced to death is Troy Dugar, who was 15 years and five months old when he committed his crime. He was sentenced to death on May 1, 1987 – his 16th birthday.

The return of the rope

In Britain capital punishment has been abolished. No one has been executed for murder for three decades. But opinion polls show that the majority of the British public would like to see "the return of the rope." Many claim that this would make some would-be murderers think twice, a view for which there is no proof. Opponents of capital punishment claim that it is barbaric, and that nothing can justify the state deliberately taking a human life. They also point to the case of Timothy Evans who was hanged for murder. After his execution, investigations revealed that Evans was in fact innocent.

"Let's do it" – the case of Gary Gilmore

In the summer of 1976, in Utah, Gary Gilmore cold-bloodedly gunned down two men. Up until that time, Gilmore had been a small-time thief who had spent most of his life in reform school and in various prisons.

Gilmore was sentenced to death. But the death penalty had been virtually abolished in the United States. The country had not executed anyone for over ten years. Normally his sentence would have been changed automatically to life imprisonment. However, Gary Gilmore insisted that the death sentence be carried out. Eventually Gilmore got his way. He was finally put to death by firing squad. His last words were "let's do it." The Gilmore case hit the headlines. Gilmore became a media star. His case crushed the hopes of those opposed to the death penalty in the United States. Since the Gilmore case more than 125 prisoners have been executed in the United States.

In the United States, as in Britain, people feel angered and frustrated by the rising tide of violent crime. This is the main reason why the death penalty is approved of by most Americans.

After 18 years in penal institutions, murderer Gary Gilmore decided he would rather be executed than spend the rest of his life in prison. But he had to fight to get his death sentence carried out.

Some politicians who were once firmly opposed to legal executions have recently changed their position to suit the public mood.

"Since 1976, when the death penalty was reinstated by the courts, 37 defendants who were black or from another ethnic minority have been executed for murdering white victims. No white offender has as yet been executed for having murdered just one white." Amnesty International report.

CASE STUDY: DOING TIME

"Keith" is in his early twenties. Since his early teens he has served time in many jails and prisons. He was recently released from Strangeways prison after serving a four-year sentence for robbing an electrical shop in Manchester, England, armed with a baseball bat.

For Keith, by far the worst aspect of Strangeways was the amount of time inmates spend "locked up" in their cells. On a normal day, Keith would spend 23 hours in a cramped cell with two other men. His only break would be a 45-minute "exercise period" – walking around the exercise yard.

A typical day
7.00 am: The bell sounds to wake the prisoners. Inmates leave their cells for a serving area to get breakfast and return to their cells to eat it. A typical breakfast consists of tea, porridge and a piece of bacon.
7.35 am: Slop-out. Keith takes out a bucket full of urine. There are no proper toilet facilities in his cell.

7.40 am: Locked up in the cell again.
11.30 am: Back to the serving area to collect dinner, which is also to be eaten in the cell. A typical dinner comprises boiled potatoes and a scoop of peas and gravy.
1.00 pm: Exercise: up to 45 minutes of walking in a circle in the exercise yard.
4.30 pm: Tea. A meal similar to dinner.
5.30 pm: Slop-out. Keith is locked up in his cell until 7.00 am next morning.
6.00 pm: A cup of tea is brought to the cell.

CHAPTER 6

ALTERNATIVES

Community service is viewed by many as a more humane method of punishment than imprisonment, and one which is more likely to reform the offender.

Why prisons?

It is usually accepted that there are always likely to be seriously violent and genuinely dangerous individuals, and such people may need to be deprived of their freedom for a very long time, for the protection of the rest of society. But prison reform groups stress that this only applies to a tiny minority. For the vast majority of offenders, a spell in prison makes a person more, not less, likely to offend again. Nearly three-quarters of all juveniles who spend time in jail are rearrested within the course of a year.

> **"Prisons are academies where the apprentice criminal can learn his trade."** Former British Home Secretary, Douglas Hurd.

But if prisons only make things worse, why does every country in the world persist in having them? One possible answer is that prisons represent the easy way out for society. What to do with difficult, destructive, antisocial people? Shutting them away in prison is a simple, convenient solution to a highly complex problem.

Prisons are dumping grounds. They are old-fashioned and ineffective. Prisons can even make things worse; they are also an increasingly expensive solution. What are the alternatives?

Tagging

The use of electronic tagging devices to track an offender's movements was invented by a judge in New Mexico who got the idea from a Spiderman cartoon. Instead of being jailed, offenders and people awaiting trial are made to wear an electronic tag. These are usually lightweight plastic bracelets that fit around the ankle. Tags emit an electronic signal which enables the authorities to know exactly where an offender is at any time. Tag-wearers usually have to accept certain restrictions on their movements. They must agree to stay at home in the evenings, for example. Or they must not leave their neighborhood. The rules vary. But if a person breaks the rules, or tries to interfere with the tag in any way, then the device will sound an alarm signal and the offender can be rearrested by the police.

Tagging is a very new experiment. Only around 12,000 offenders in the United States are currently being tagged. But already there have been many criticisms. Tagging has been called degrading. It has been described as the modern version of the ball and chain that convicts once wore.

Tagging can turn a person's home into a prison. In Britain, one young offender chosen for a tagging experiment quickly tore off the device, saying he did not want to be a guinea pig, and would rather go to prison!

For another offender in the United States convicted of driving offenses, "prison" was a black box that picked up radio signals emitted every 30 seconds from a transmitter strapped to his leg. If he tried to remove it or interfere with it in any way, real prison beckoned.

"I hear that box and I feel like tearing it from the wall. All this for driving with a suspended licence." Tagged offender.

Community service

Instead of going to prison an offender can be invited to perform a certain benefit to the community – decorating a retirement home, or helping to build an adventure playground for children are two examples.

The range of people who may perform community service orders is very wide. They include top sports stars such as Mike Tyson, the World Heavyweight boxing champion, and Mark Gastineau, the New York Jets defensive end. Tyson spent his time visiting youth centers in poor neighborhoods urging the kids to "stay on at school and get an education." Gastineau taught football skills to young jail inmates to fulfill his

Tasks allotted to offenders on community service may include work in parks, garbage collection, and duties at youth centers.

90-day community service order resulting from a conviction for assault.

Probation

There are many different kinds of probation. Under the supervision of a probation officer, for example, an offender may be asked to take part in a program of education and training, or asked to seek medical help.

Victim reparation programs

An offender who has stolen from a neighbor may be required to agree to work under the supervision of a probation officer to pay back the victim for the damage and distress he or she has caused. Most reparation programs involve small amounts. But sometimes they can assume larger proportions. For example, one offender was sentenced to three years in prison for stealing $160,000 from her place of work. The sentence was suspended for an alternative reparation/restitution package that combined over 700 hours of community service at a girls' home with a repayment order of $300 a month for 28 years.

Helping offenders help themselves

"Many people who get into serious difficulties have a lot of potential. At 17, 18, 19 and 20, that's the time people are having to test themselves, prove themselves. You have got to find ways that respond to that level of activity." Probation Officer.

VisionQuest

In the United States, the VisionQuest juvenile treatment program for offenders includes wilderness survival training, rock climbing, and a three-month sailing voyage. The rearrest rate for VisionQuest graduates is 32 percent in the first year of freedom, compared with 75 percent in youth custody.

"VisionQuest is not a job, it's a lifestyle."
Robert Burton, Founder of VisionQuest.

In Norway, Sweden and Denmark, there are many programs for offenders that attempt to cure rather than punish them. In Norway, for example, 1,500 people who have got into trouble because of drugs and alcohol have been sent on a mountaineering course. As the course instructor puts it, "If they want to get high let them get high up a mountain!"

Young offenders in the uniform of the US cavalry are put through their drill during the innovative VisionQuest program. The project staff are highly dedicated, and youths are treated as family members rather than "offenders."

CHAPTER 7

CRIMES AGAINST HUMANITY

War criminal Klaus Barbie was tried in France in 1985. Estimates of the number of deaths he ordered reached as high as 30,000. The punishment of those who have committed crimes against humanity poses a great challenge to judicial systems internationally.

"Ordinary people do not know that every kind of evil is possible." Concentration camp survivor.

There are times when everyone would agree that harsh punishment is inevitable. At the end of World War II, as the German occupation of Europe was pushed back by the allied armies, clear evidence of extreme cruelty committed by the Nazi forces on a massive scale began to emerge. Thousands of cases were fully documented by the allies with sworn statements by witnesses, as well as film and photographic evidence. A permanent record of Nazi atrocities was formed that could never be dismissed as being faked "war propaganda."

These records together reveal "the most terrible crime in history," the deliberate destruction of six million European Jews, as well as homosexuals, disabled people, Gypsies, Slavs, and other nationalities who were systematically rounded up and exterminated throughout a network of concentration camps.

To deal with the sheer immensity of such crimes, a new category of criminality had to be invented – the crime of genocide, the crime against humanity. The arrest and prosecution of those responsible continues. In January 1984, 40 years after the war's end, Klaus Barbie, an elderly German, was arrested in Bolivia on charges of fraud and organizing paramilitary groups. But investigators also discovered that Barbie had been a high-ranking Nazi during the war, and was wanted in France, where he had twice been sentenced to death in his absence for war crimes committed during his time as head of the notorious Nazi secret police, the Gestapo.

France demanded his extradition and Barbie was sent back to Lyon to face trial for crimes committed 40 years earlier. In July 1985, Barbie was finally convicted in France and sentenced to life imprisonment. Barbie had personally ordered the torture and murder of thousands of men, women and children. Among his victims were young children from a Jewish orphanage.

Many war criminals like Barbie took refuge in Britain, the United States and Canada. In Britain there are moves to bring them to trial. But many feel that it is impossible to try people fairly for crimes committed over 45 years ago.

The trial of the Ceausescus

On Christmas Day 1989, the dictator of Romania, Nicolae Ceausescu, and his wife, Elena, were executed by a firing squad after being found guilty by a military tribunal of "crimes against the people," including genocide. The trial lasted a few hours and was broadcast on television. The Ceausescus were executed soon after.

The Ceausescu dictatorship had lasted 24 years. It was a cruel and brutal regime. Millions suffered. But the Ceausescus did not receive a "fair trial." Was the trial and execution of the Ceausescus a just punishment?

SOURCES OF HELP

American Correctional Association
8025 Laurel Lakes Court
Laurel, MD 20707

National Center on Institutions and Alternatives
1165 Harrison Street
San Francisco, CA 94103

National Coalition Against The Death Penalty
1419 V Street, N.W.
Washington, DC 20009

American Civil Liberties Union
132 W. 43 Street
New York, NY 10036

Criminal Justice Statistics Association
444 N. Capitol Street, N.W.
Suite 606
Washington, DC 20001

In addition, various state Departments of Corrections may provide help and information.

GLOSSARY

acquitted found not guilty by a jury.

bail to obtain the release from custody of someone by putting up money as a guarantee.

convicted found guilty by a jury.

custody imprisonment.

deterrent a punishment that puts people off crime.

discharged set free by the court.

felony a crime that is considered more serious than a petty crime.

martial law rule by the army.

offender a person who commits an offense against the law.

rehabilitation restoring a person's good character.

retribution taking vengeance.

sentence the decision of the court as to the punishment of an offender.

vigilante a person who takes it upon himself to dispense justice.

FACTFILE

People in prison in the United States

America's prison population has been increasing yearly for the last 16 years. The total number of state and federal prisoners in the United States in 1989 was 703,687, the highest number ever.

Percentage by race in 1988

White   35
Black   47.8
Hispanic   16
Other   1
(American Indian, Asian, Pacific Islanders, Eskimos)

Percentage by gender

Male   94.4
Female   5.6

Housing the prison population

U.S. prisons suffer from chronic overcrowding. The number of inmates has tripled since 1975. It is estimated that there are about 60,000 more than the system was designed to hold. Thirty-five states are under court order to relieve overcrowding; 27 states have population caps set by federal courts. In New York City, prisoners are housed on two surplus ferryboats and two converted British troop barges.

A five-story floating jail is under construction. California, with an inmate population of 80,721, the largest number of prisoners in the United States, is spending $3.2 billion on more space. It costs $16 billion a year to house all the prisoners. The average cost of $24,800 would pay for room, board, and tuition at the country's best colleges.

Death Row

More than 2,300 prisoners are on death rows around the country, and their numbers increase nearly every week as the appeals process blocks executions and more killers are convicted. Thirty-six states have capital punishment statutes.

Since the 1976 U.S. Supreme Court ruling allowing states to resume use of the death penalty, over 125 people have been executed. From 1984 through 1989, an average of 19 people a year were executed.

INDEX

Photographic Credits